PIANO SKILLS

SIGHT-READING

STEPHEN GEARRY

ZEBRALINE
PUBLISHING

First edition, 2009 by Zebraline Publishing

Printed in England by Caligraving Ltd

ISBN 978-0-9562500-0-1

Published by Zebraline Publishing
Email: zebraline@europe.com

www.zebralinemusic.co.uk

ABOUT THE SERIES

Three years in the making, **Piano Skills** truly is an innovation in piano tuition, designed for use in lessons and also for reference at home. Each book focuses on one of five key areas of piano study: Theory, Sight-reading, Dexterity, Interpretation, and Practice - and this structures the method of learning into a flexible yet organised format. Each book may be used in sequence (Book 1 through to 5) or in combination to specifically target weak areas, and furthermore, 'simultaneous learning' is still an option for teachers but with the added benefit of independent study available for the student.

Dedicated to the beginner, only white notes are used throughout the whole series, and a fully proven, user-friendly interface of *five-note sets* (see centre pages) ensures a high rate of learning, crucial for building confidence in the early stages.

The concept of five-note sets aims to encourage methodical use of finger notation by providing an easy system with which to catalogue and emphasise the simplicity of five-note hand positions to the beginner, and this system enables the student to learn exercises quicker as a result of musical material being presented as pre-analysed.

Logical structure, direct writing style, clear layout, and polished melodic content all serve to make the first steps in music as rewarding as possible. Enjoy!

ABOUT THE AUTHOR

Stephen Gearry is an accomplished pianist, teacher, and composer with over 15 years of musical experience. After graduating at the University of Hull with 1st-class honours in music he has dedicated himself to the development of the **Piano Skills** resource.

In 2006, he was awarded the *Andrew Brown Memorial Prize in Music* for distinction in solo piano performance and is also on the judging panel for the Nottinghamshire Young Pianist of the Year.

Having received tuition from 1st-class Moscow Conservatoire graduate, Irina Glushenkova, he has since appeared in masterclasses with established artists such as Neil Immelman, Richard Meyrick, and Sarah Briggs.

CONTENTS

SECTION 1

Sight-reading Concepts

An introduction to the concepts of sight-reading

Sight-reading Concepts

Generally speaking, the fundamental concept of sight-reading is to follow instructions as directed. This introductory chapter explores the process of sight-reading and the relative mental skills used. Below is a chronological sequence of events which occurs during the process of sight-reading:

Recognition	–	understand the information
Coordination	–	convert the information
Action	–	execute the information

Recognition

The ability to recognise pitch and rhythm fluently on the score is vital to the success of your sight-reading. Before recognition can occur, familiarity of pitch and rhythmic notation on the score must first be acquired.

Ideally, the recognition of note-names and rhythms on the stave should be instant. Aim for the same speed of fluency as reading words and numbers.

Coordination

After understanding an instruction, instant coordination of your actions in response will take time and practice to perfect, which is why it is so important to practise sight-reading every day. Always remember that regular sight-reading will improve your success.

Your first attempt to respond to the following instructions will simulate the stage of practising coordination:

1. Pat your head with one hand (up and down movement), and rub your stomach with the other (circular movement).
2. Point both index fingers towards each other and rotate them in opposite directions – one clockwise, one anti-clockwise.
3. Whilst sitting, lift your right foot off the floor and draw clockwise circles with it. At the same time draw the number '6' in the air with your right hand.

Action

The desired end-result of sight-reading is merely the correct response to instructions.

Test your fluency of recognition, coordination and action by following the instructions as outlined below to simulate the general concept of sight-reading.

In the following grids you must execute your actions *steadily*, following the instructions from left to right, row by row.

CLAP	**Instructs to clap**
B	**Instructs to say 'blue'**
G	**Instructs to say 'green'**
R	**Instructs to say 'red'**
Y	**Instructs to say 'yellow'**

START HERE →

G	CLAP	Y	B
CLAP	R	CLAP	G
B	Y	B	CLAP
R	G	CLAP	R

START HERE →

CLAP	B	Y	G
R	Y	CLAP	B
B	CLAP	R	G
Y	G	B	CLAP

START HERE →

B	R	Y	G
G	CLAP	B	CLAP
CLAP	Y	CLAP	R
R	B	G	Y

SECTION 2

Pitch

Pitch relates to the names of notes

Treble Clef

The following exercises develop note recognition and 'playing by interval' in the treble clef. The exercises in this section are not melodic and so rhythm and tempo are completely free. To begin an exercise, place your right hand within any of the five-note sets (see centre pages) and play the notes as directed. Repeat the exercises with your left hand, remembering to practice equally with each hand.

These exercises may be turned upside-down for further tests in the bass clef.

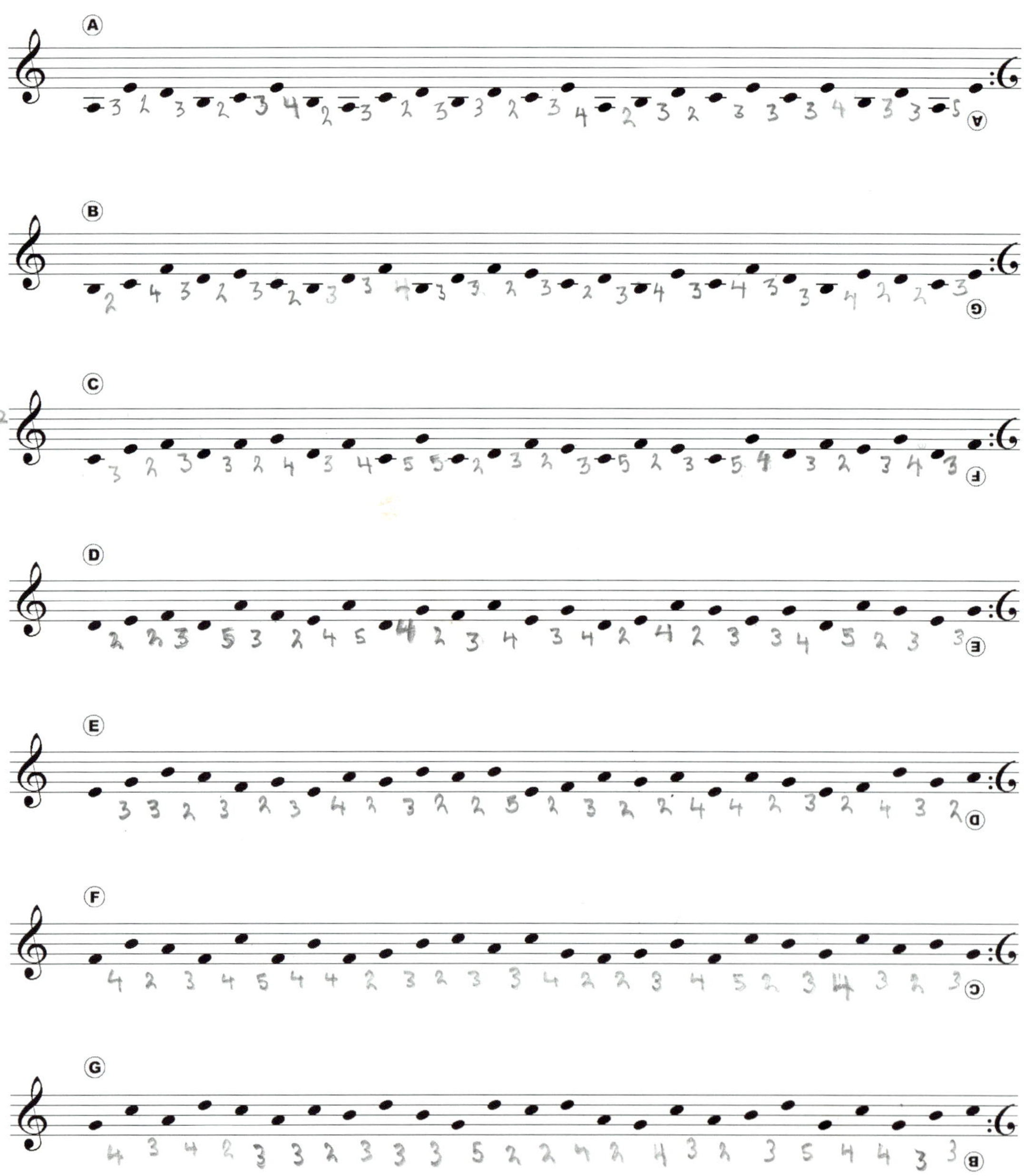

Treble Clef – Octave Higher

The following pitch exercises are an octave higher for further tests of note recognition.

These exercises may be turned upside-down for further tests in the bass clef.

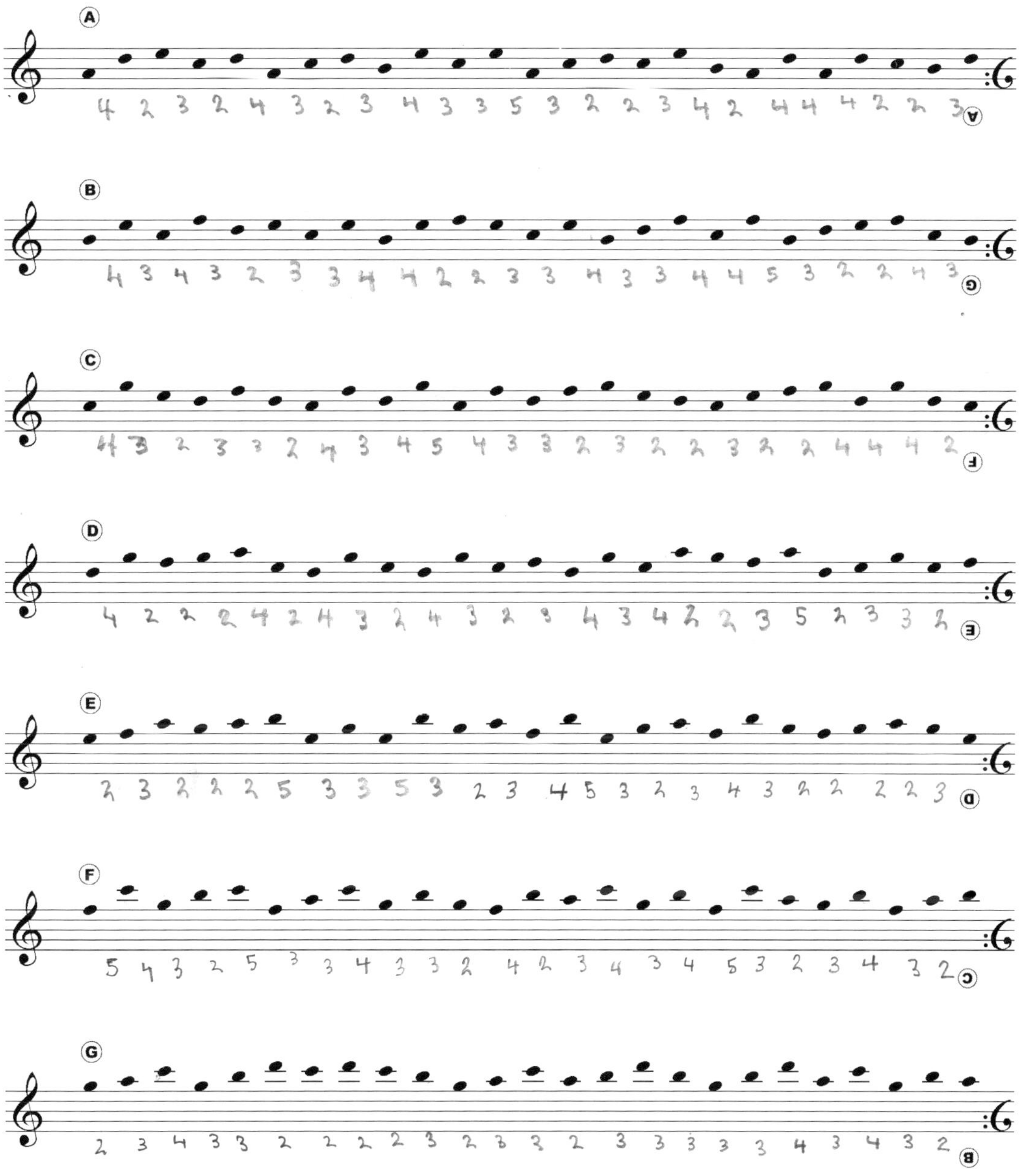

Bass Clef

The following exercises develop note recognition and 'playing by interval' in the bass clef. The exercises in this section are not melodic and so rhythm and tempo are completely free. To begin an exercise, place your left hand within any of the five-note sets (see centre pages) and play the notes as directed. Repeat the exercises with your right hand, remembering to practice equally with each hand.

These exercises may be turned upside-down for further tests in the treble clef.

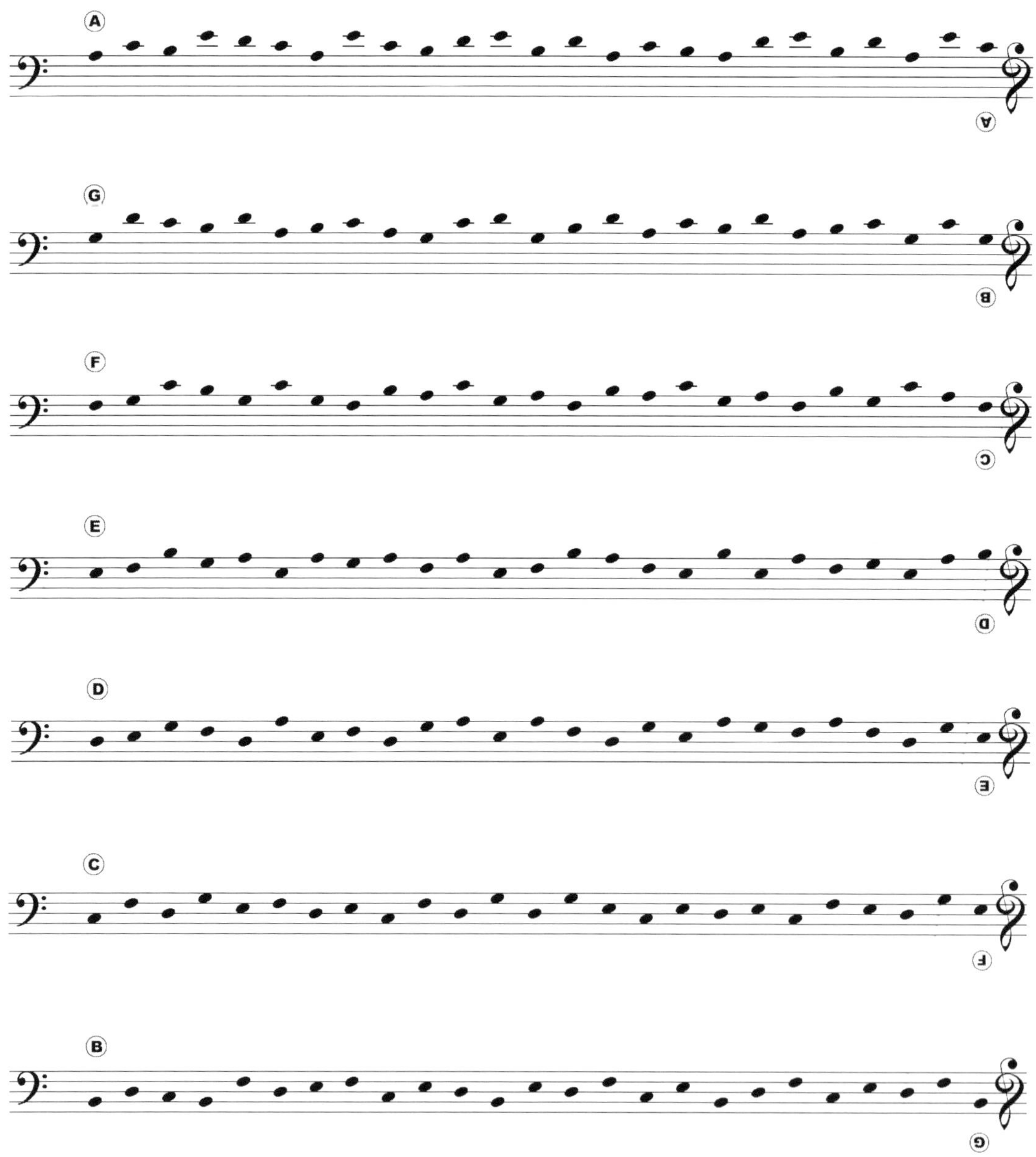

Bass Clef – Octave Lower

The following pitch exercises are an octave lower for further tests of note recognition.

These exercises may be turned upside-down for further tests in the treble clef.

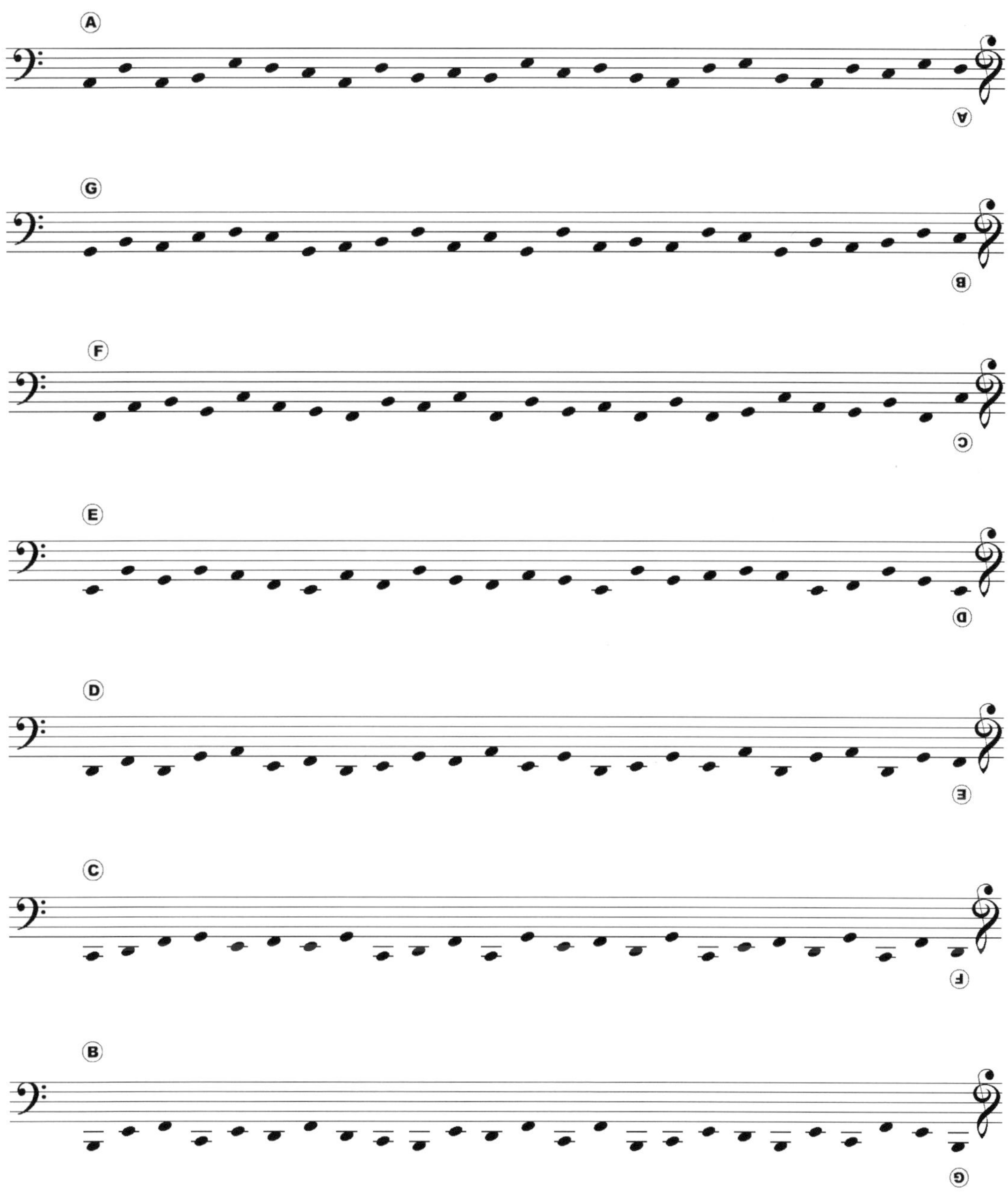

SECTION 3

Rhythm

Rhythm relates to the time duration given to each note

Beat Boxes

Beat Boxes are user-friendly visual aides to assist with the understanding of rhythmic notation. Here is an example of a Beat Box grid:

Bar 1	1	2	3	4
Bar 2	1	2	3	4
Bar 3	1	2	3	4
Bar 4	1	2	3	4

Each row in the grid represents one bar of four beats, denoting the time signature, $\frac{4}{4}$. When using a Beat Box grid, all grey areas represent sound, whereas the white areas represent silence.

Grey - Instructs a clap

White - Instructs silence

Rhythm Staves

Rhythm staves have only one line upon which note values are placed to notate rhythm.

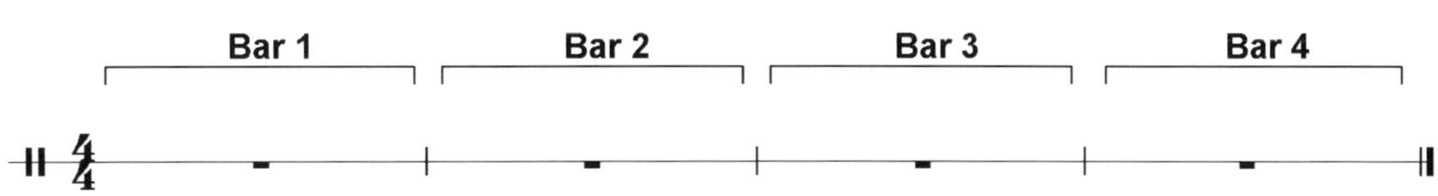

For all exercises in this section clap the rhythms of each Beat Box as instructed and then clap the same rhythm on their respective rhythm stave.

Crotchets

Crotchet

Crotchet rest

Exercise 1

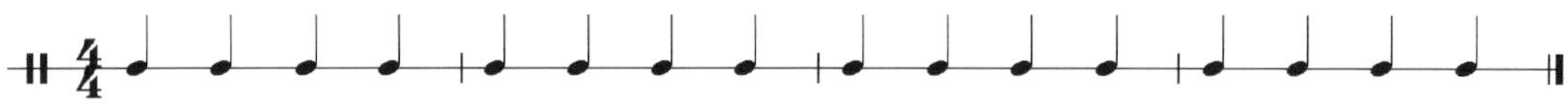

1	2	3	4
1	2	3	4
1	2	3	4
1	2	3	4

Exercise 2

1	2	3	4
1	2	3	4
1	2	3	4
1	2	3	4

Exercise 3

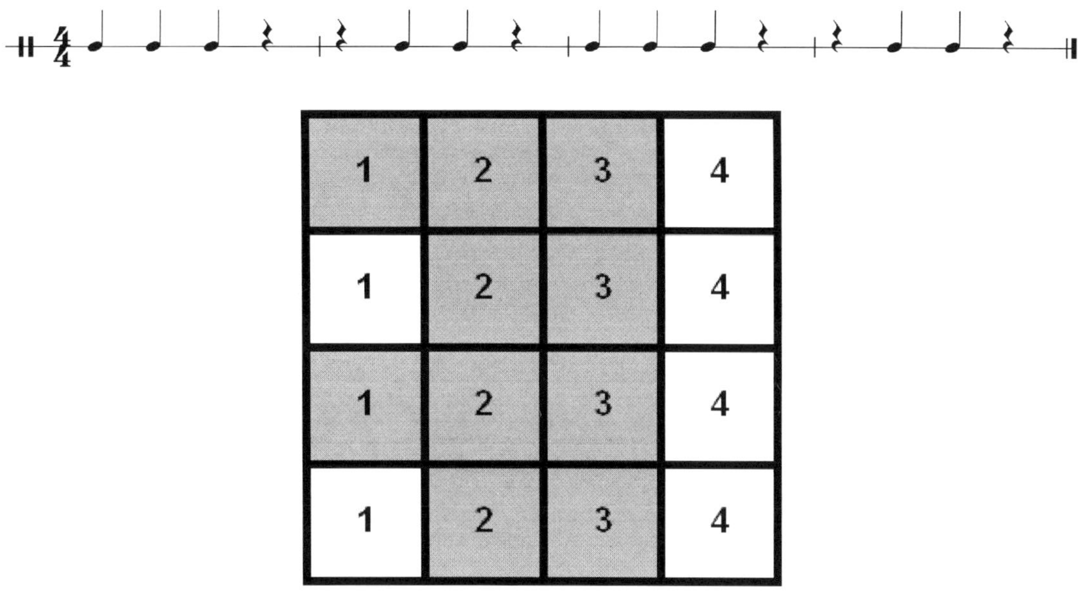

Exercise 4

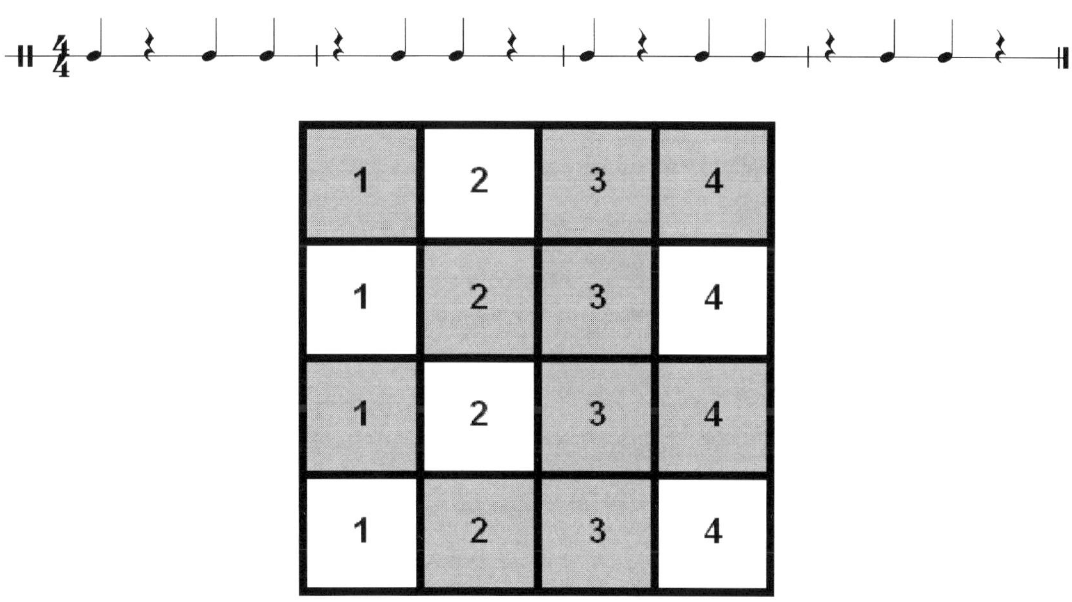

Exercise 5

1	2	3	4
1	2	3	4
1	2	3	4
1	2	3	4

Minims

 **Minim**

 **Minim rest**

When boxes are merged, hold the sound for the length of all boxes concerned:

1 2

Two beats of sound

1 2

Two beats of silence

Exercise 1

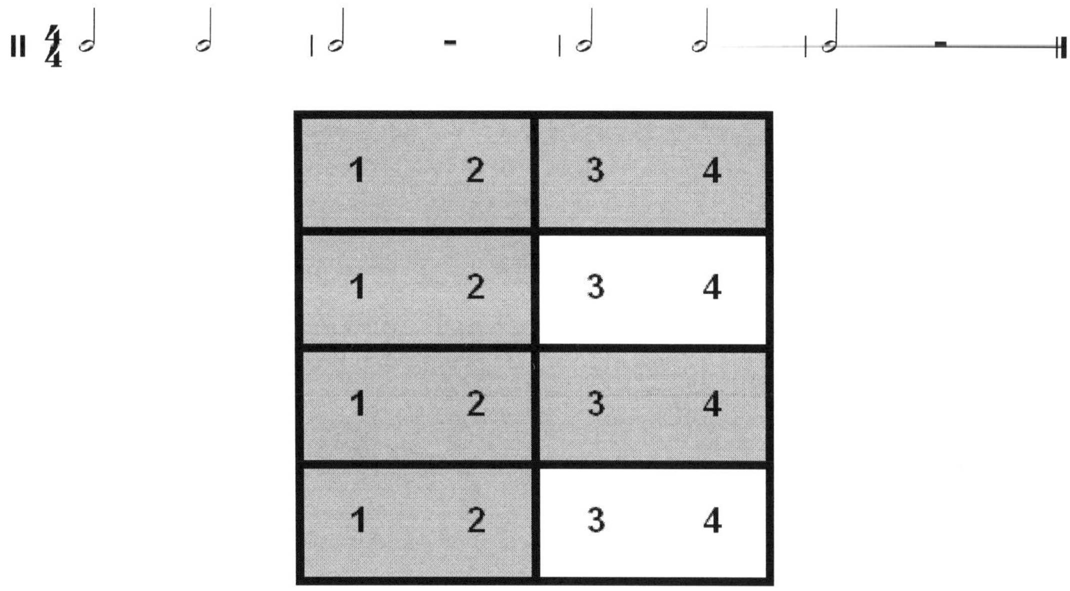

Exercise 2

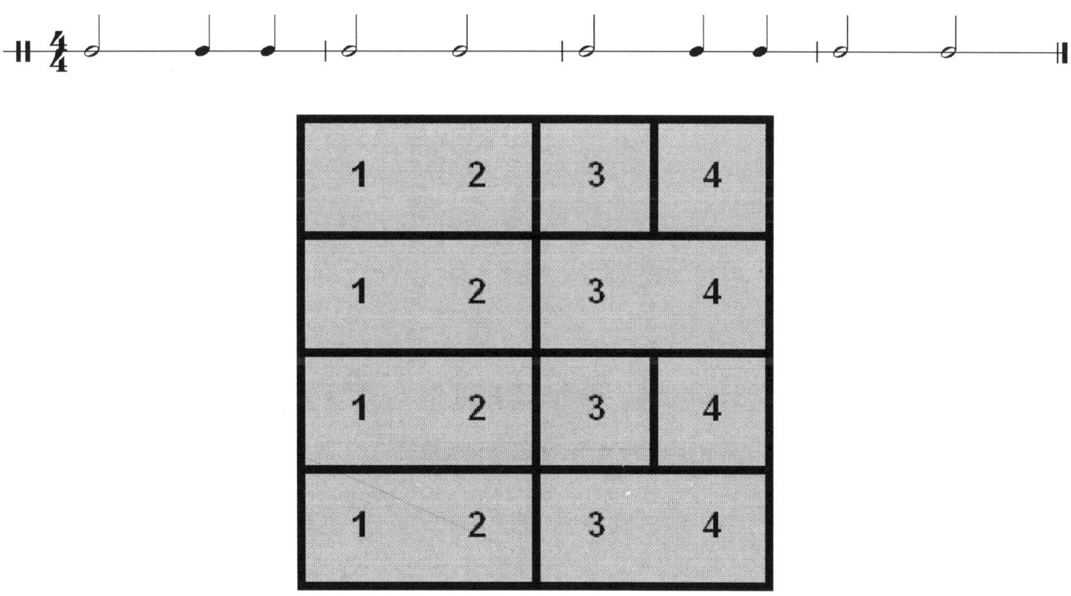

Exercise 3

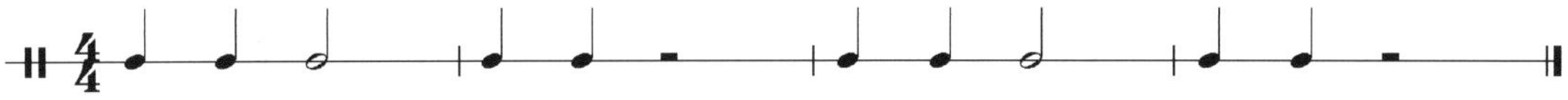

1	2	3	4
1	2	3	4
1	2	3	4
1	2	3	4

Exercise 4

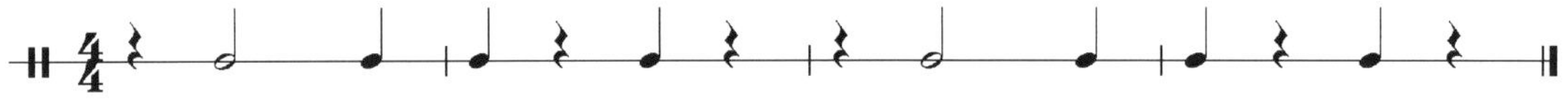

1	2	3	4
1	2	3	4
1	2	3	4
1	2	3	4

Exercise 5

1 2	3	4
1 2	3	4
1 2	3	4
1 2	3	4

Semibreves

Semibreve

Semibreve rest

Exercise 1

1 2 3 4
1 2 3 4
1 2 3 4
1 2 3 4

Exercise 2

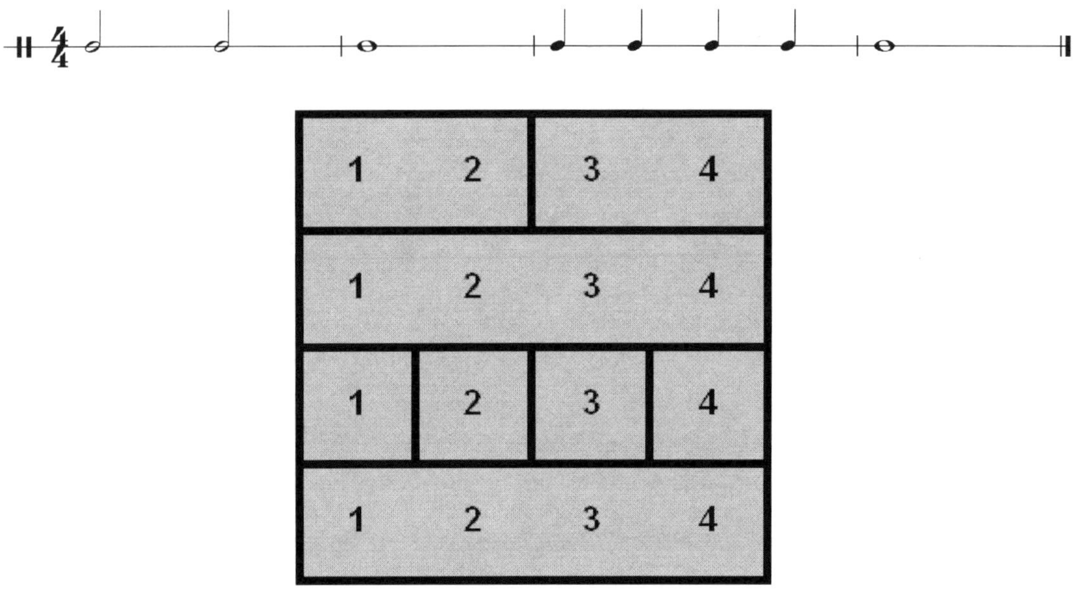

Exercise 3

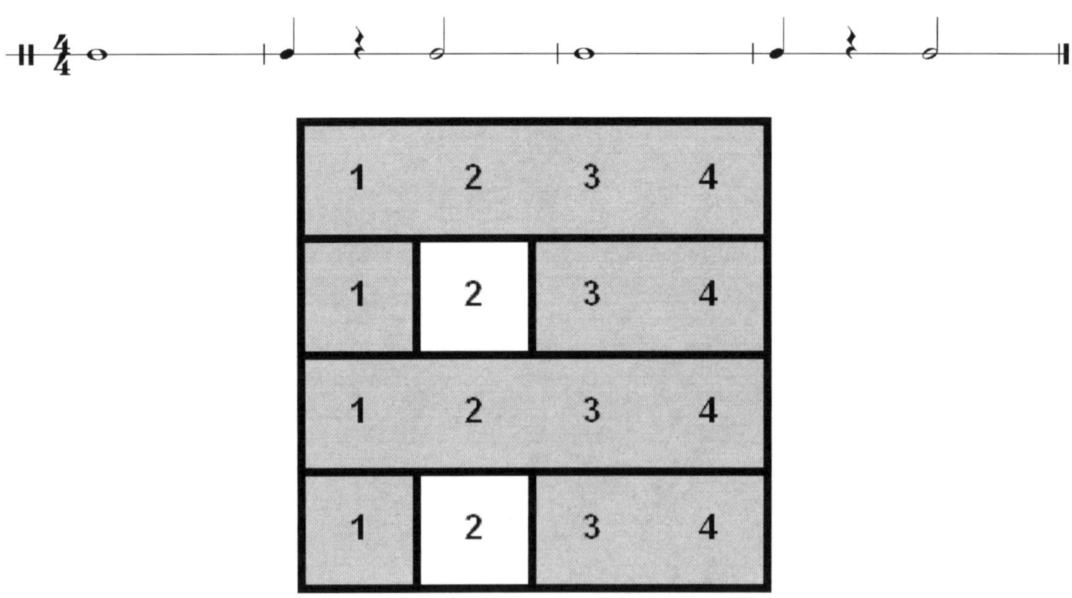

Exercise 4

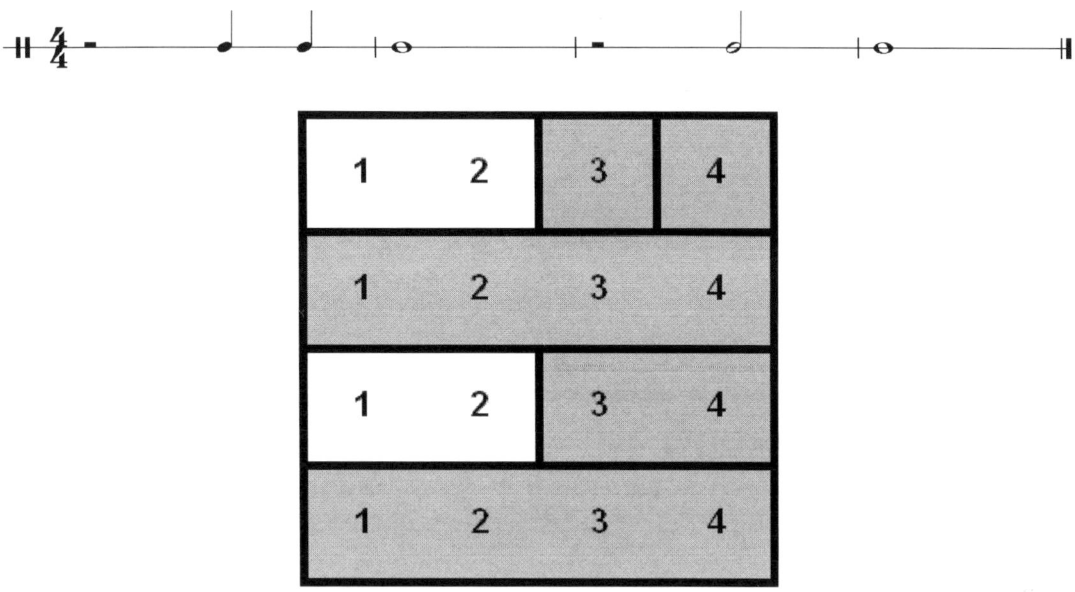

Exercise 5

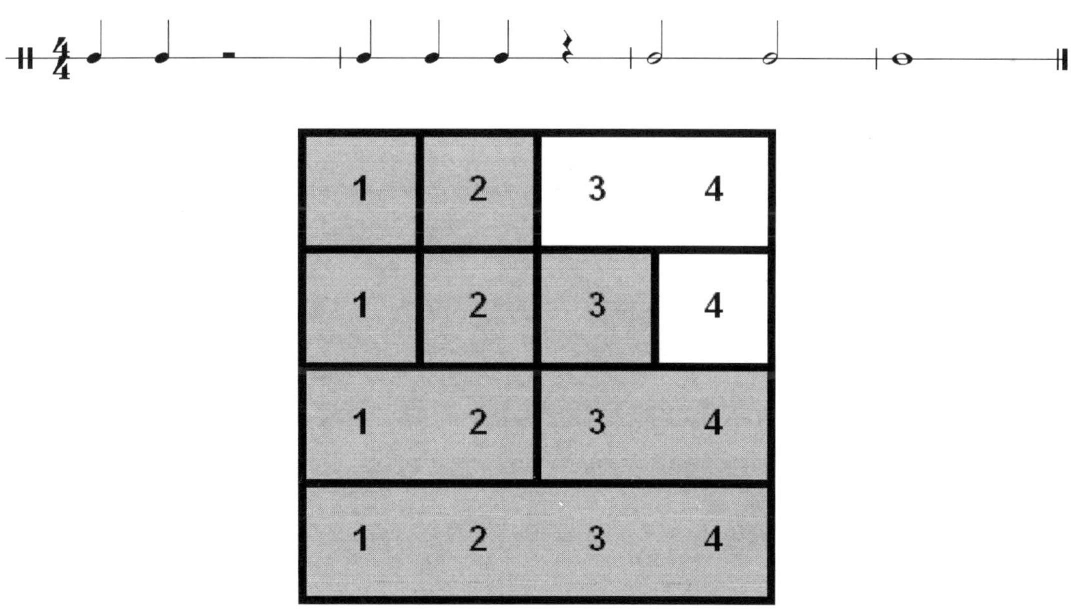

Ties

Tie

Ties connect two note values together to create one single note value. For most of the time, ties are used to connect notes across barlines in order to extend the maximum note length in a bar.

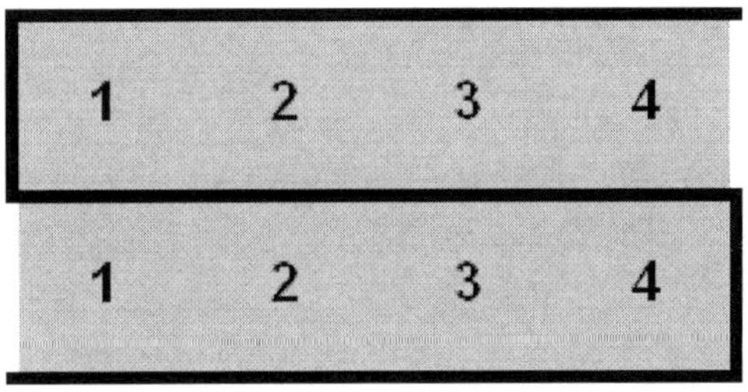

→ Hold sound into the next bar

Exercise 1

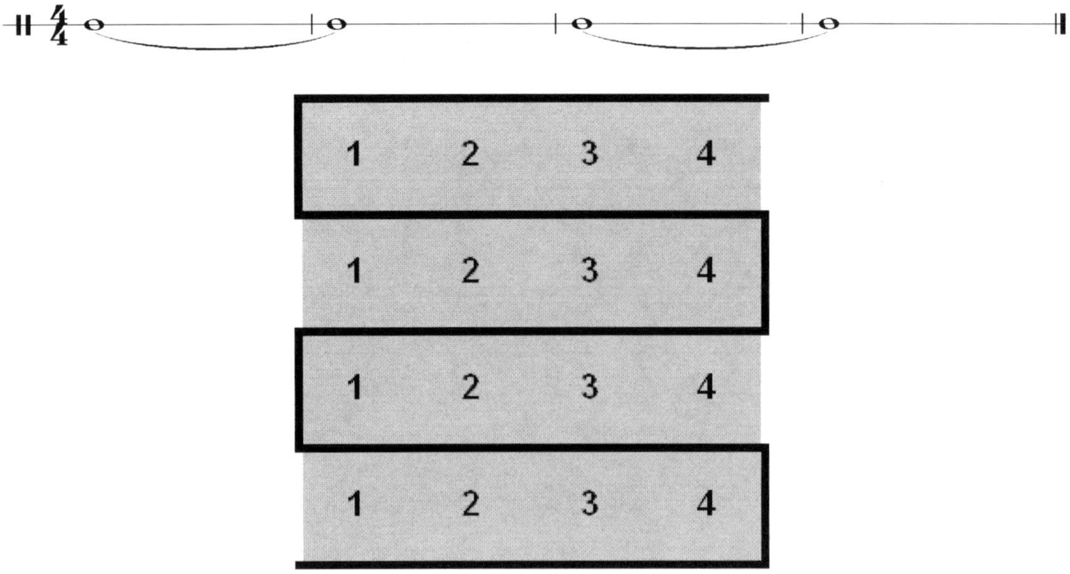

Exercise 2

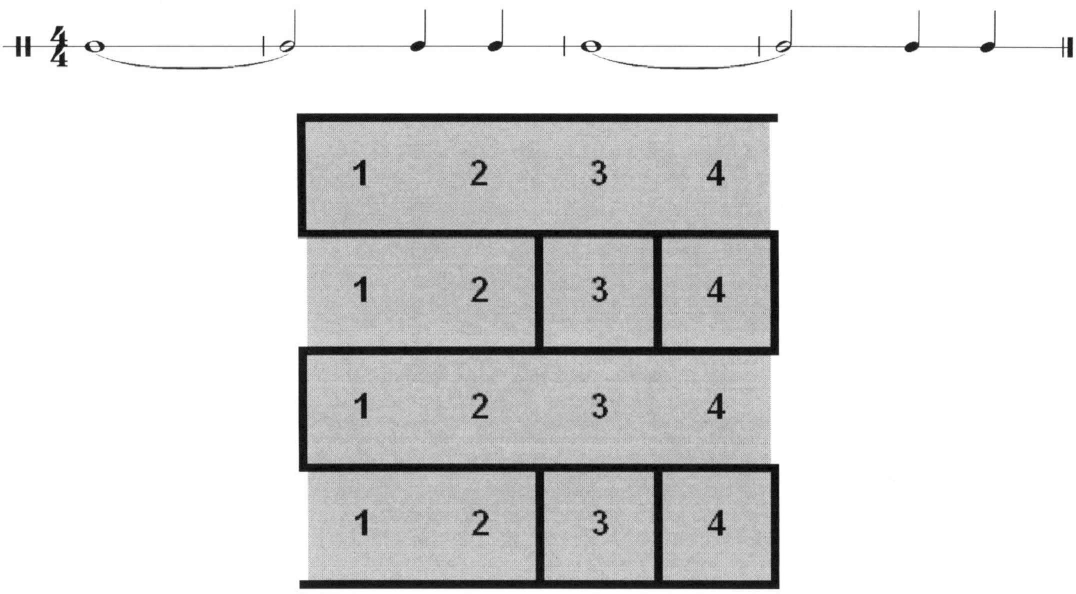

Exercise 3

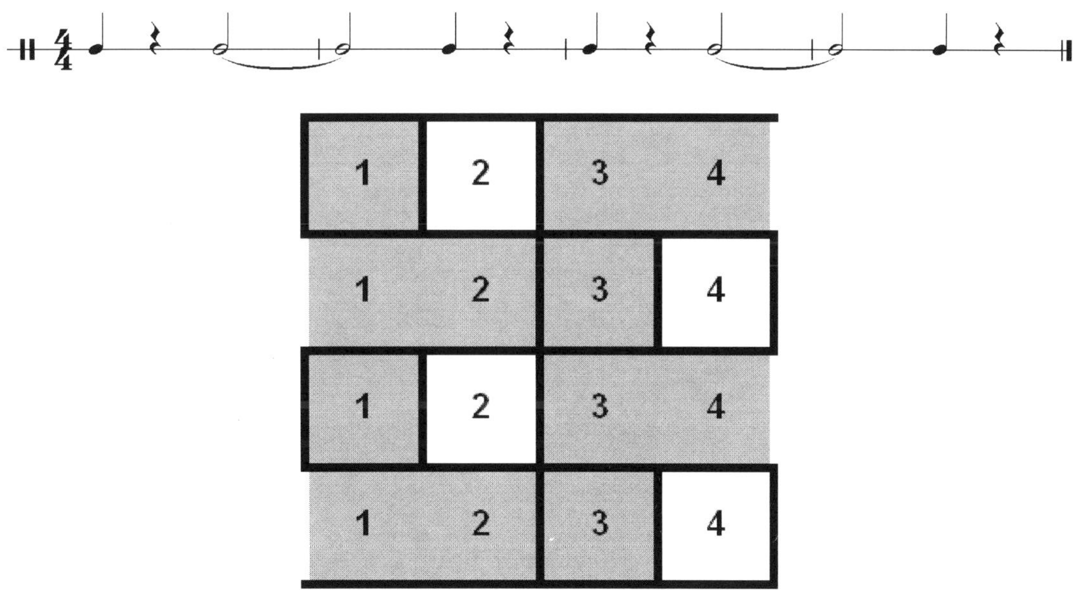

Exercise 4

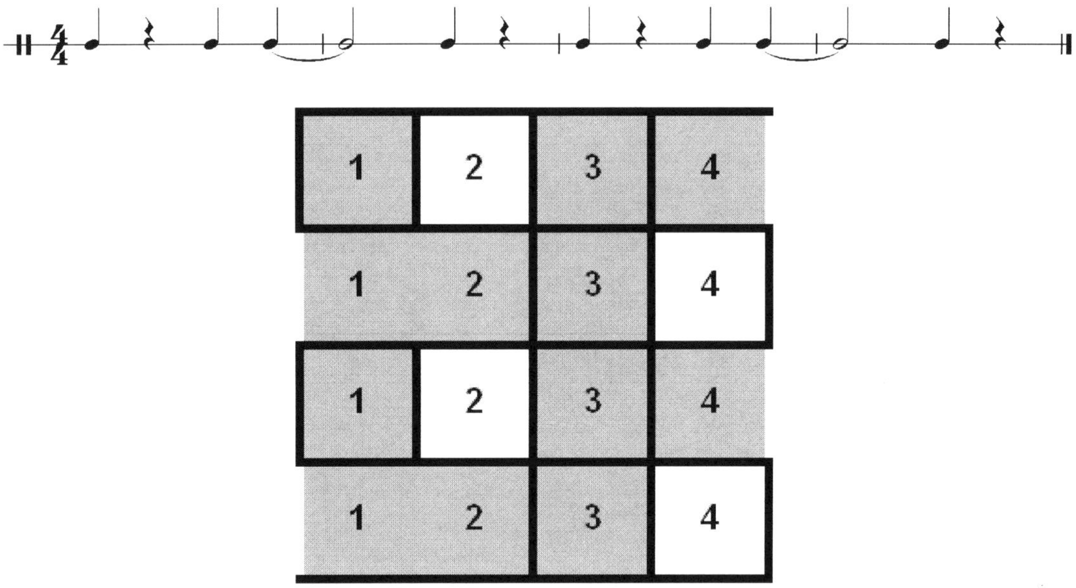

Exercise 5

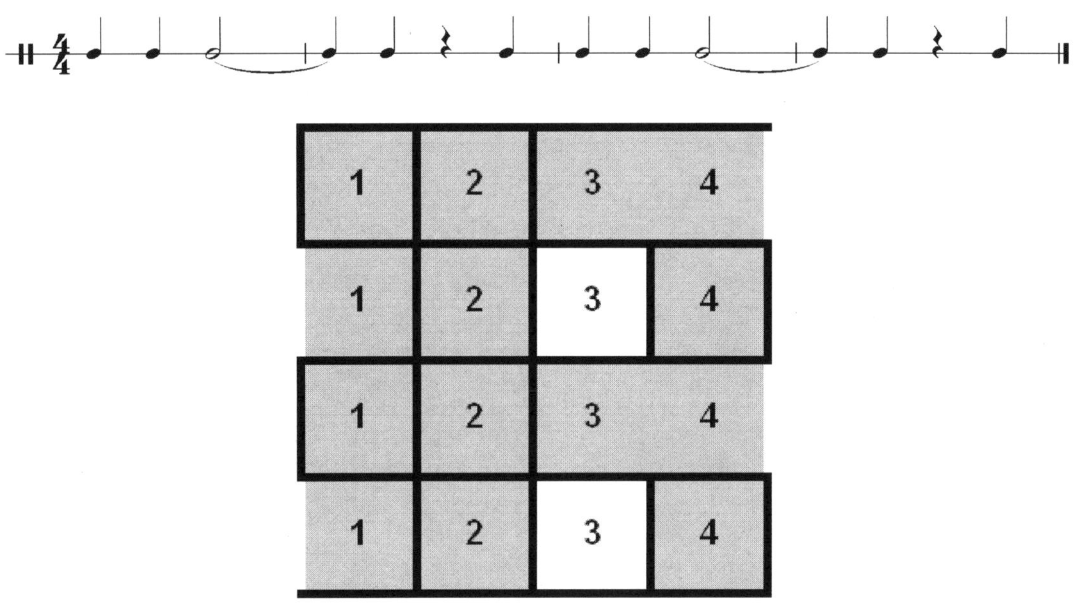

Quavers

 Quaver

 Quaver rest

1	+

= 2 quavers

1	+	2	+	3	+	4	+

= 8 quavers

The '+' symbol above instructs you to visualise (or say) the word 'and' halfway between the numbered beats – "1 and 2 and 3 and 4 and" – this enables you to keep track of where each beat should fall.

Exercise 1

<table>
<tr><td colspan="2">1</td><td colspan="2">2</td><td colspan="2">3</td><td colspan="2">4</td></tr>
<tr><td>1</td><td>+</td><td>2</td><td>+</td><td>3</td><td>+</td><td>4</td><td>+</td></tr>
<tr><td colspan="2">1</td><td colspan="2">2</td><td colspan="2">3</td><td colspan="2">4</td></tr>
<tr><td>1</td><td>+</td><td>2</td><td>+</td><td>3</td><td>+</td><td>4</td><td>+</td></tr>
</table>

Exercise 2 ✓

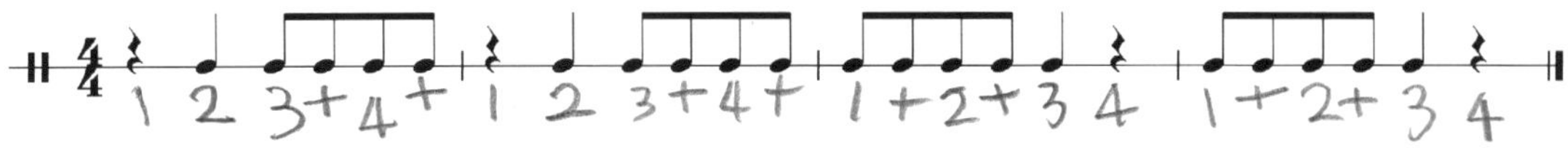

<table>
<tr><td colspan="2">1</td><td colspan="2">2</td><td>3</td><td>+</td><td>4</td><td>+</td></tr>
<tr><td colspan="2">1</td><td colspan="2">2</td><td>3</td><td>+</td><td>4</td><td>+</td></tr>
<tr><td>1</td><td>+</td><td>2</td><td>+</td><td colspan="2">3</td><td colspan="2">4</td></tr>
<tr><td>1</td><td>+</td><td>2</td><td>+</td><td colspan="2">3</td><td colspan="2">4</td></tr>
</table>

Exercise 3 ✓

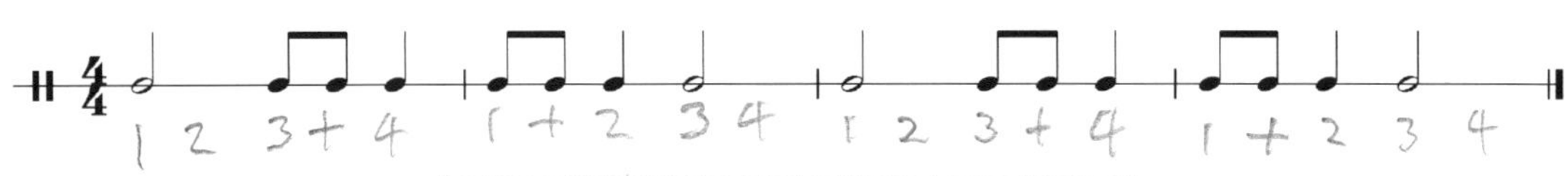

<table>
<tr><td colspan="4">1 2</td><td>3</td><td>+</td><td colspan="2">4</td></tr>
<tr><td>1</td><td>+</td><td colspan="2">2</td><td colspan="4">3 4</td></tr>
<tr><td colspan="4">1 2</td><td>3</td><td>+</td><td colspan="2">4</td></tr>
<tr><td>1</td><td>+</td><td colspan="2">2</td><td colspan="4">3 4</td></tr>
</table>

Exercise 4

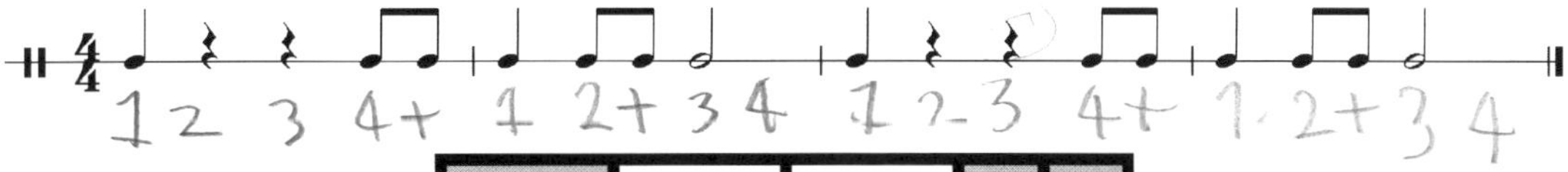

1	2	3	4	+
1	2	+	3 4	
1	2	3	4	+
1	2	+	3 4	

Exercise 5

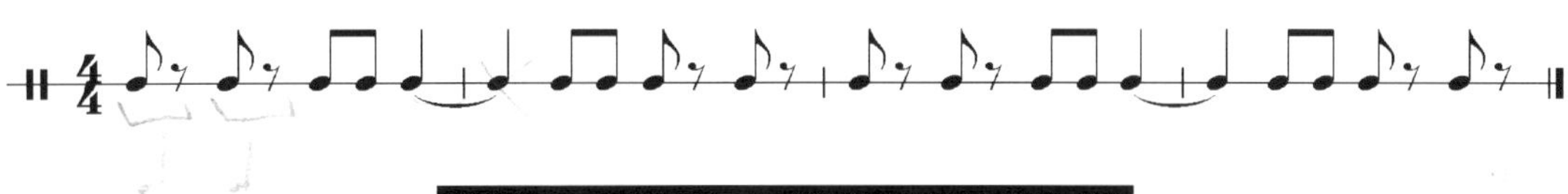

1	+	2	+	3	+	4
1	2	+	3	+	4	+
1	+	2	+	3	+	4
1	2	+	3	+	4	+

Dotted Notes

 **Dotted crotchet**

 **Dotted crotchet rest**

 **Dotted minim**

 **Dotted minim rest**

A dot placed after a note extends its length by one half of its original length.

Exercise 1

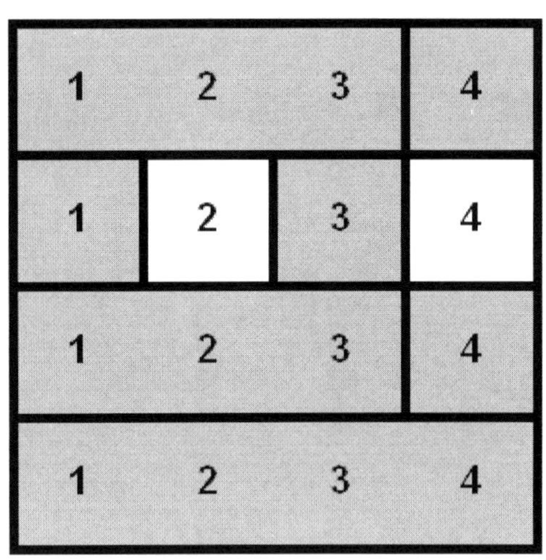

CENTRE PAGES

Five-note Sets

Finger notation and hand positions explained

LEFT HAND

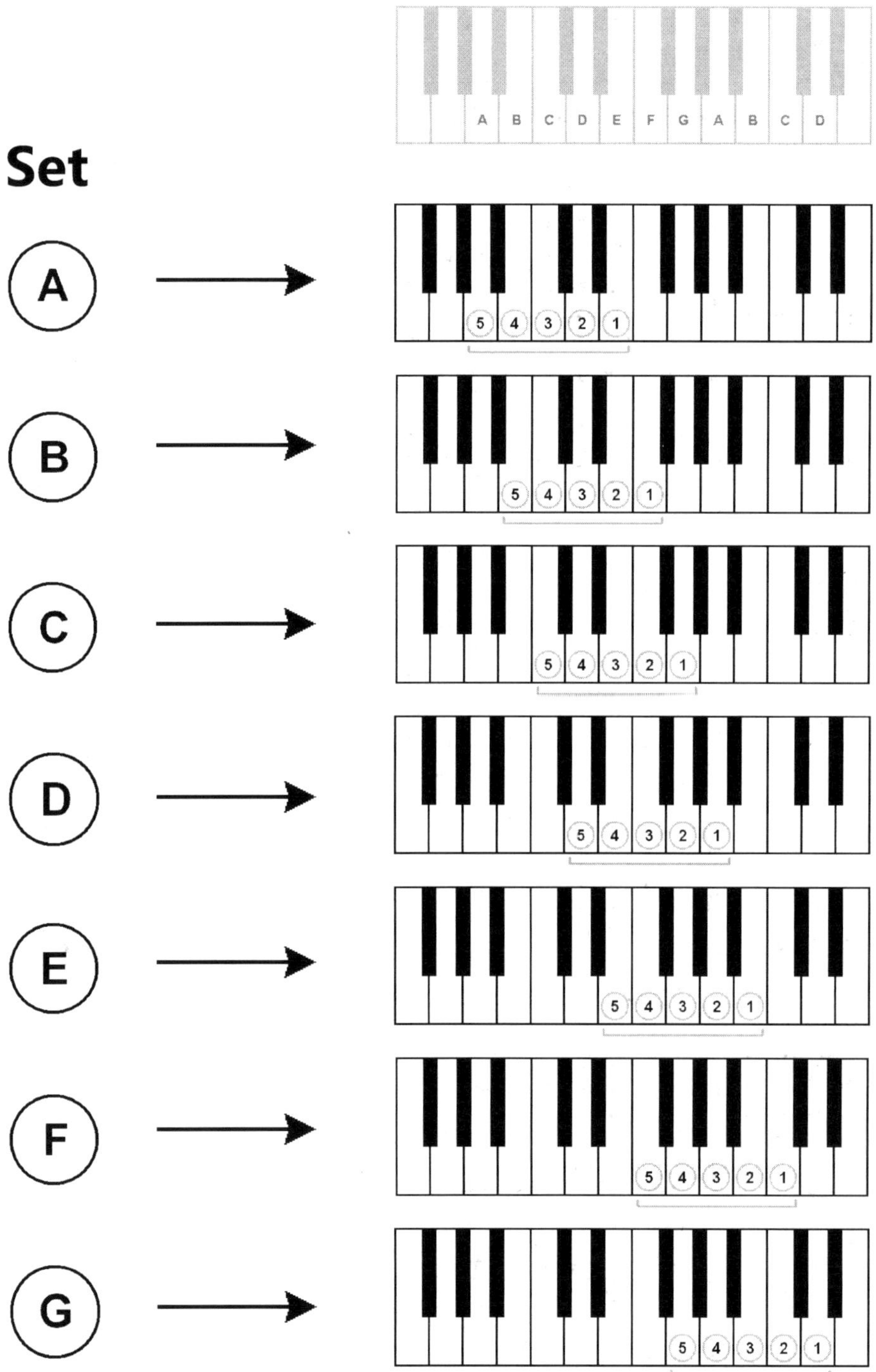

In **finger notation** (or fingering) each finger is represented by a certain number, as shown on both hand diagrams. On a score, a number above or below a note indicates the best possible finger to use for that note.

RIGHT HAND

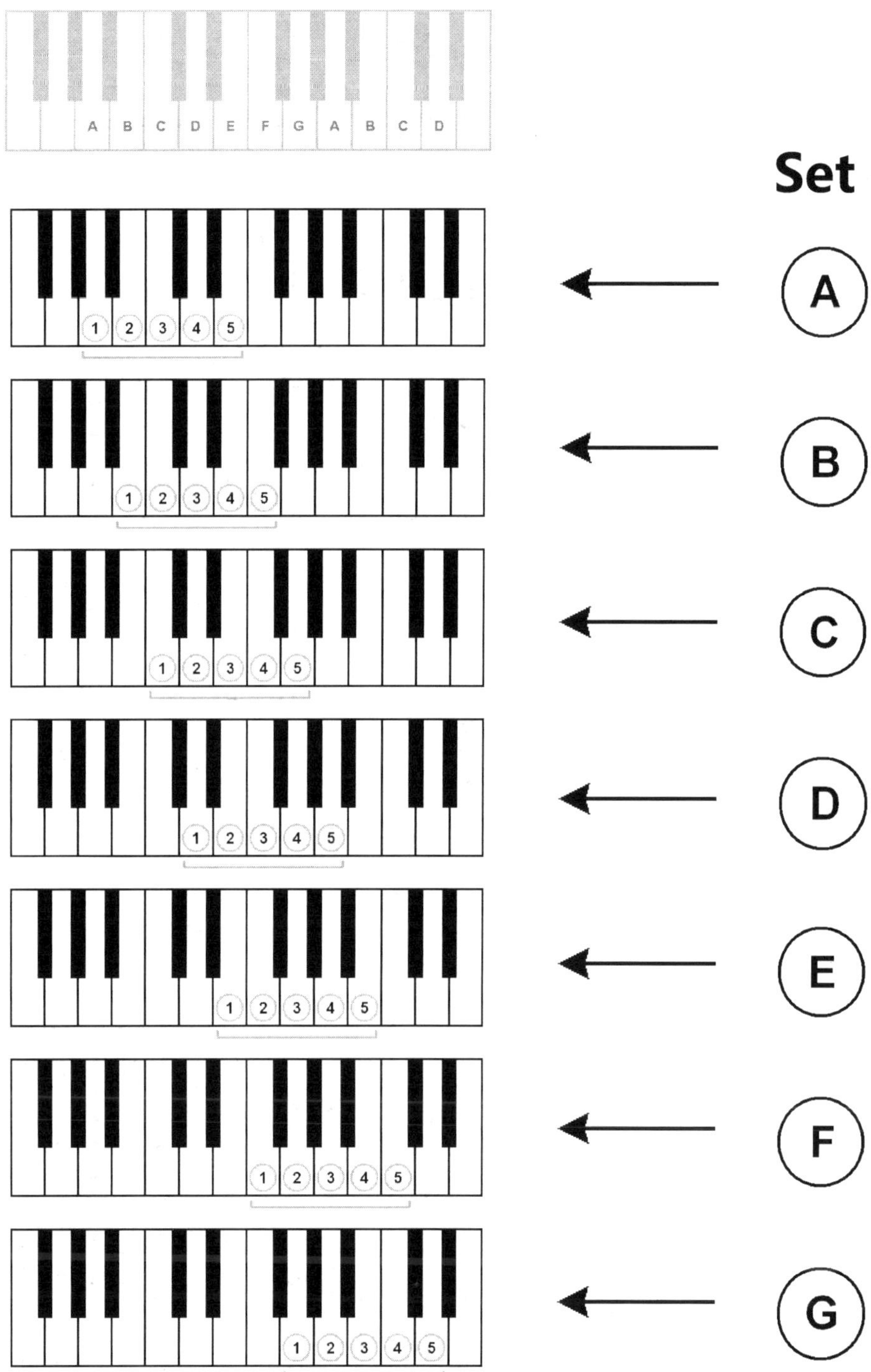

A **five-note set** is a hand position on the keyboard which comprises five adjacent white notes. A system of circled letters is used throughout this book series to indicate which hand position (or set) to assume when playing in any particular score. Numbers shown on the keyboard diagrams above represent the position of each finger within each set. Circled letters are not used for recurrently stepwise changes of five-note sets.

CENTRE PAGES

Five-note Sets

Finger notation and hand positions explained

Exercise 2

1	+	2 3 4
1 2 3	4	+
1	+	2 3 4
1 2 3	4	+

Exercise 3

1	2	+	3	4	+
1 2	+	3	4		
1	2	+	3	4	+
1 2	+	3	4		

Exercise 4

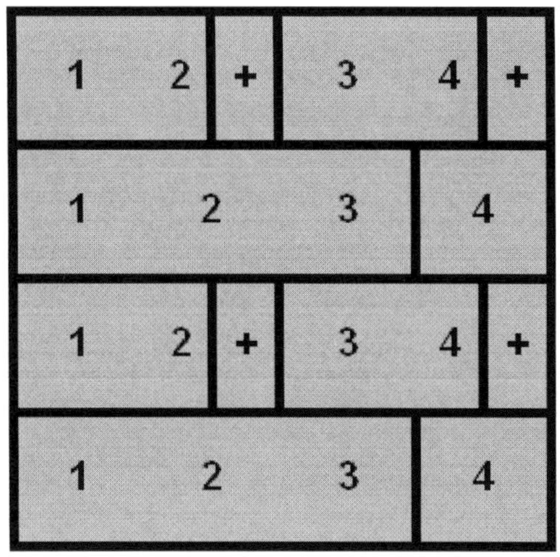

Exercise 5

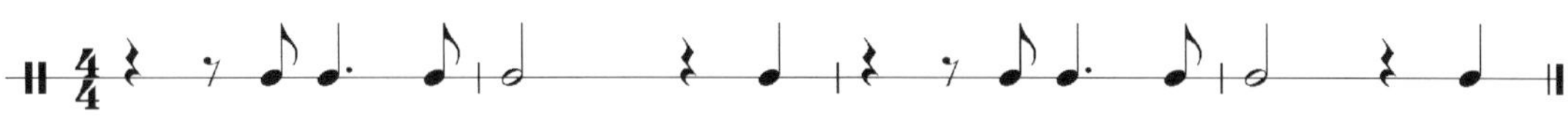

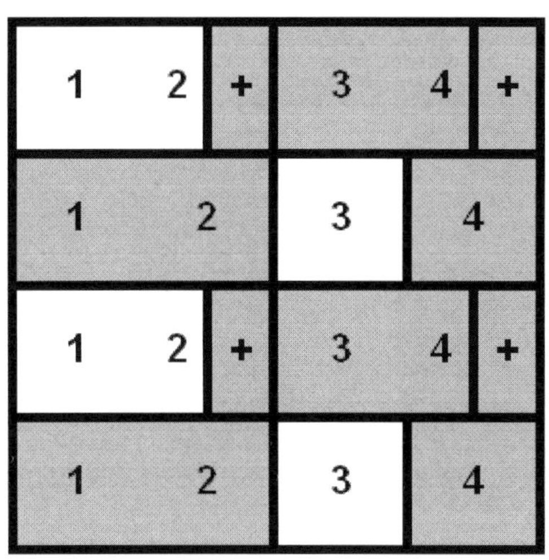

Semiquavers

Semiquaver

Semiquaver rest

Beats can be further subdivided into four smaller rhythms, known as semiquavers:

= 4 semiquavers

Exercise 1

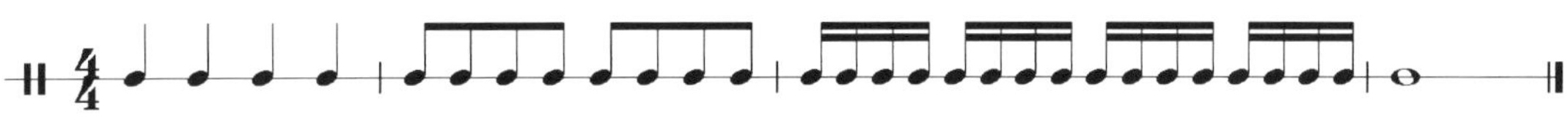

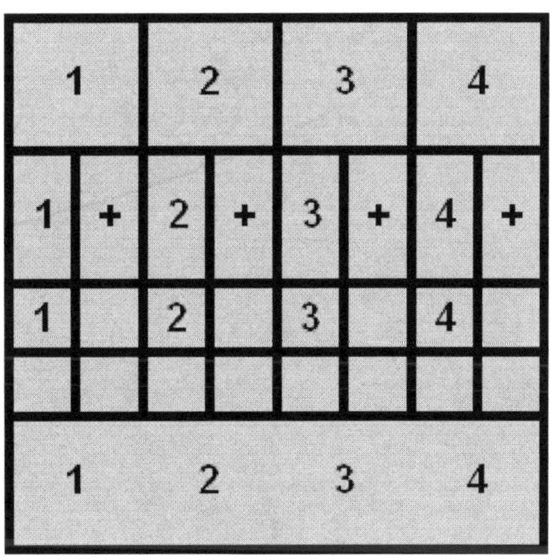

Exercise 2

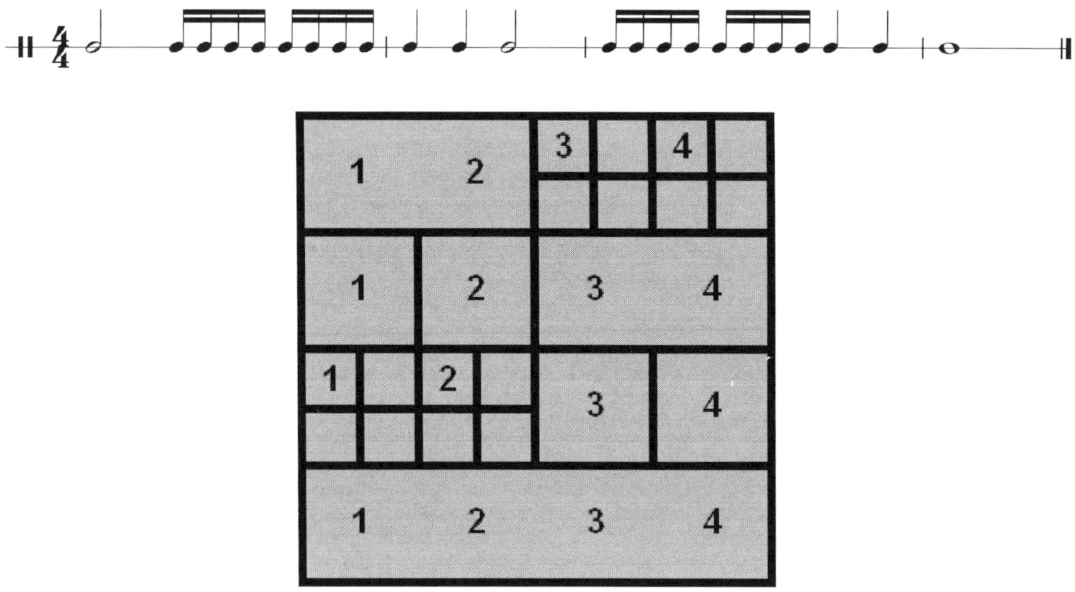

Exercise 3

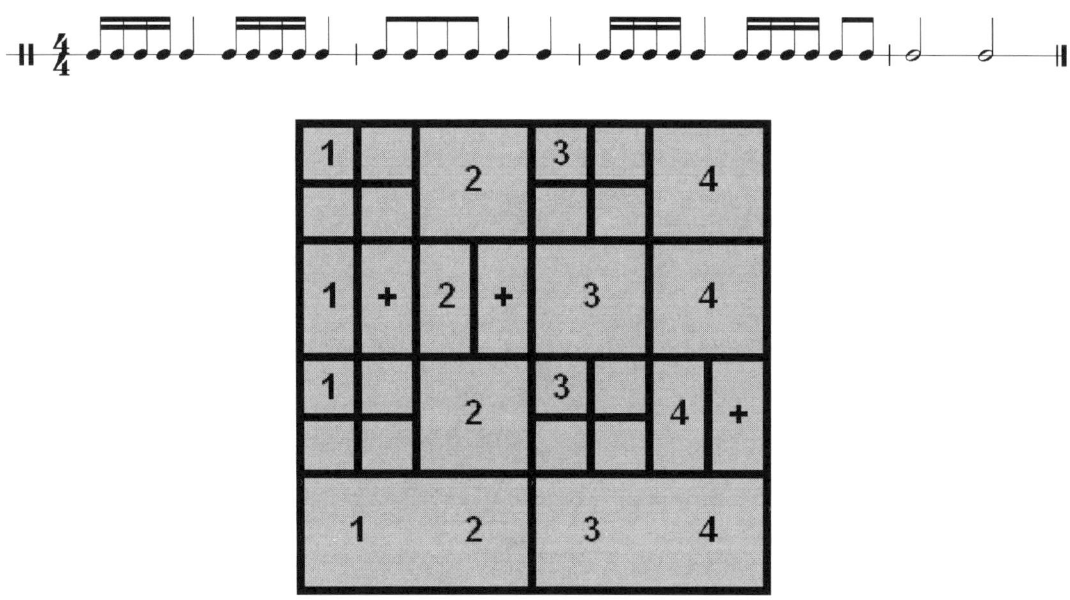

Exercise 4

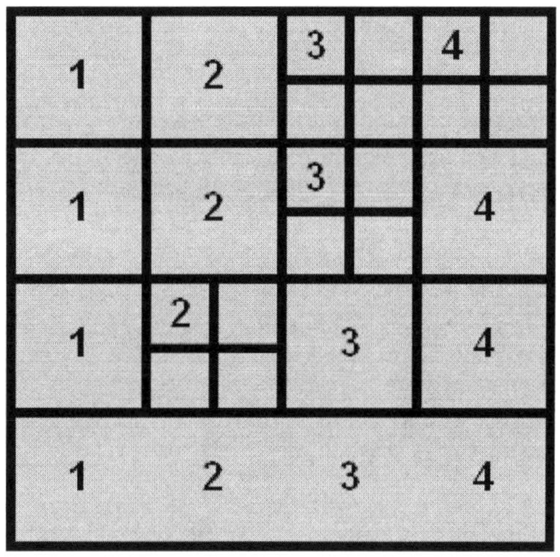

Exercise 5

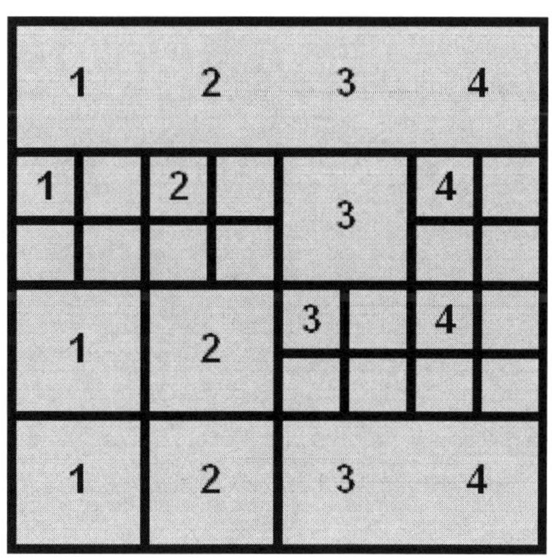

Time Signatures

Examples of **simple time** are shown below:

4 3 2
4 4 4

In simple time, the beats subdivide into twos. For example, a crotchet beat will divide into a group of two quavers:

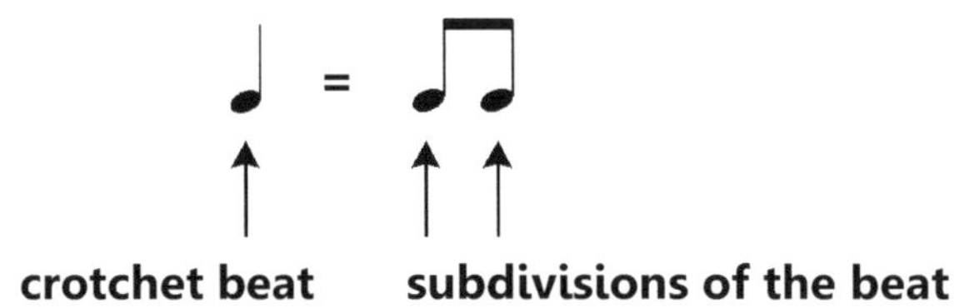

Exercise 1

4
4

1		2		3		4	
1	+	2	+	3	+	4	+
1		2		3		4	
1		2		3		4	

Exercise 2

3
4

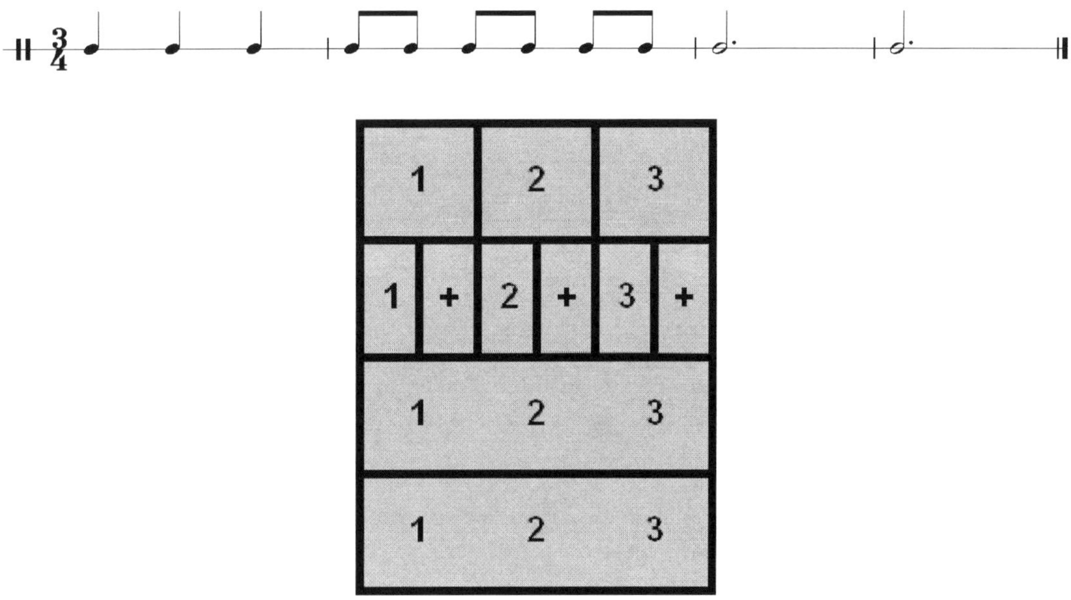

Exercise 3

2
4

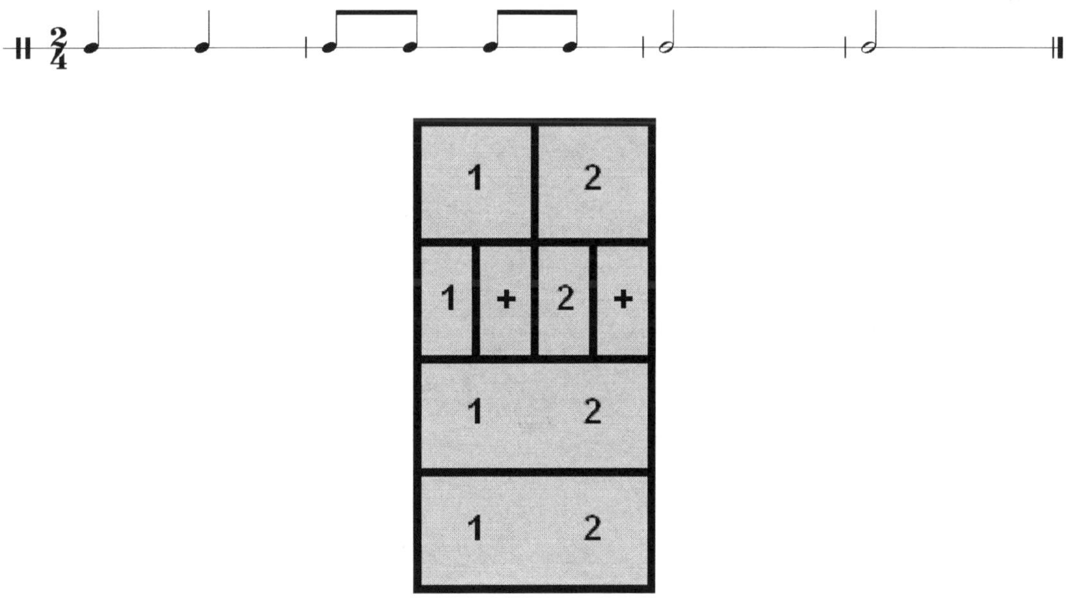

Examples of **compound time** are shown below:

6 3
8 8

In compound time, the beats subdivide into threes. For example, a dotted crotchet beat will divide into a group of three quavers:

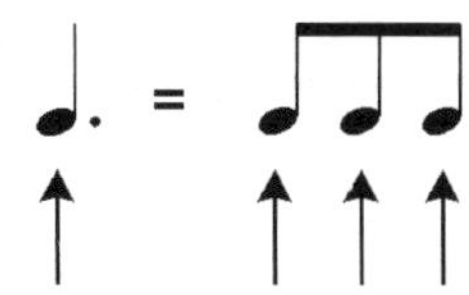

dotted crotchet beat **subdivisions of the beat**

Exercise 4

6
8

1	2	3	4	5	6
1	2	3	4	5	6
1	2	3	4	5	6
1	2	3	4	5	6

Exercise 5

3
8

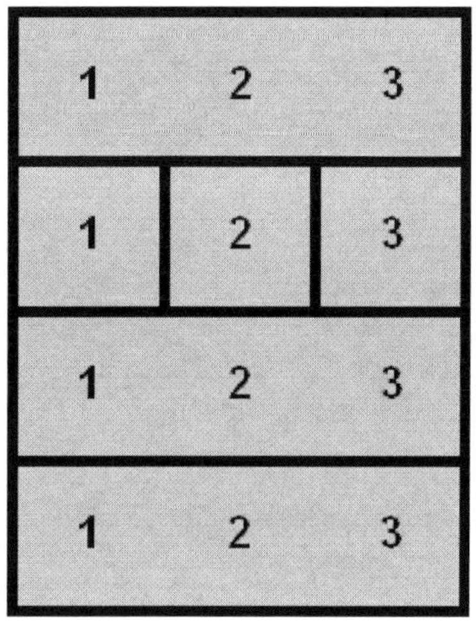

Beat Box Exercises

Create a Beat Box grid from the rhythm stave in each exercise. Shade in the correct areas and write in each beat number. Make sure to use a pencil in order to make corrections as necessary. Answers are given on page 63.

Exercise 1

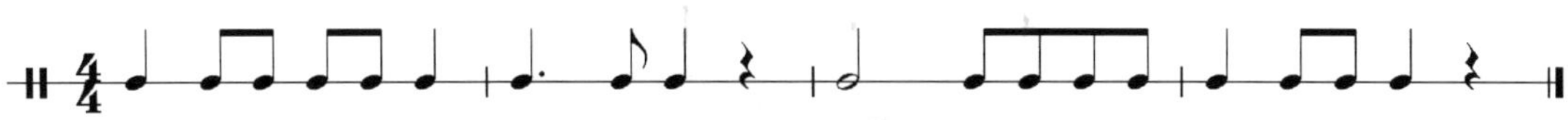

1	2+	3+	1
1	2+	3	4
1	2	3+	4+
1	2+	3	4

Exercise 2

1	2	3
1	2	3+
1	2	3
1	2	3

Exercise 3

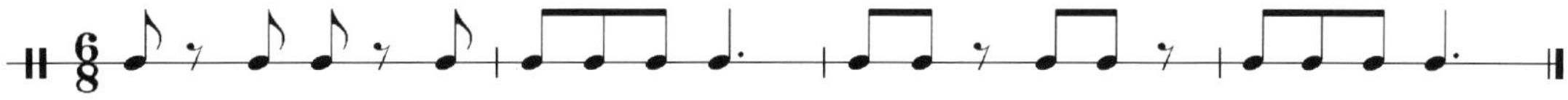

1	2	3	4	5	6
1	2	3	4	5	6
1	2	3	4	5	6
1	2	3	4	5	6

Exercise 4

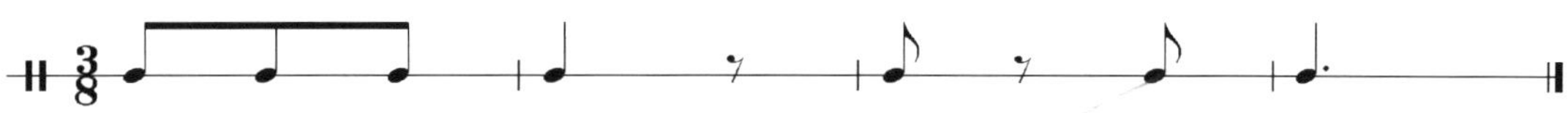

1	2	3
1	2	3
1	2	3
1	2	3

Exercise 5

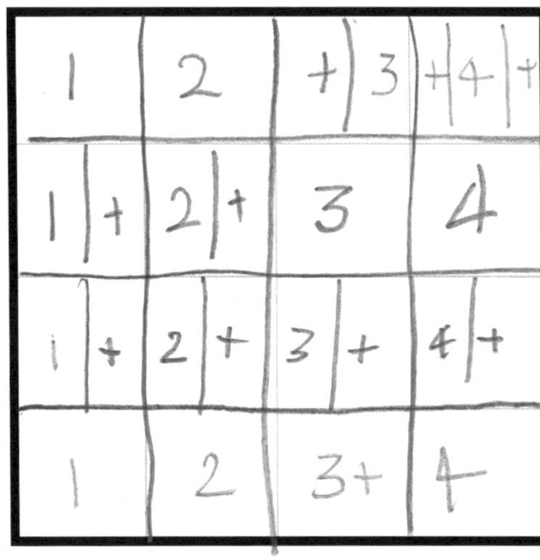

Rhythm Stave Exercises

Create a rhythm stave from the Beat Box grid in each exercise. Answers are given on page 63.

Exercise 1

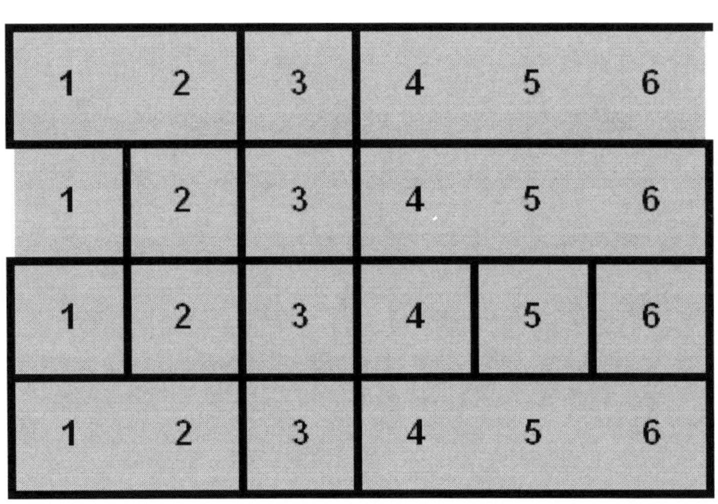

Exercise 2

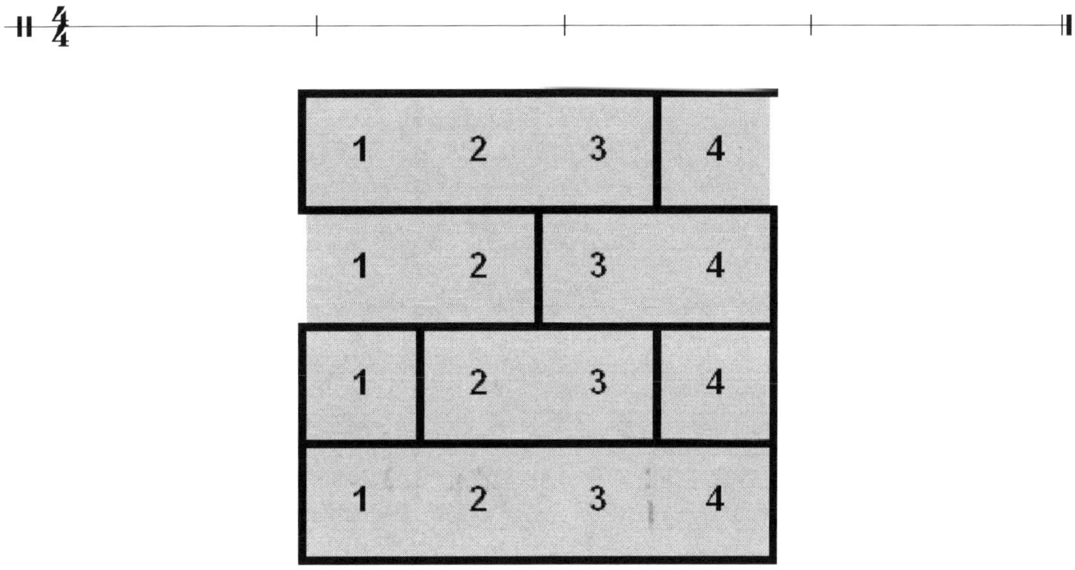

Exercise 3

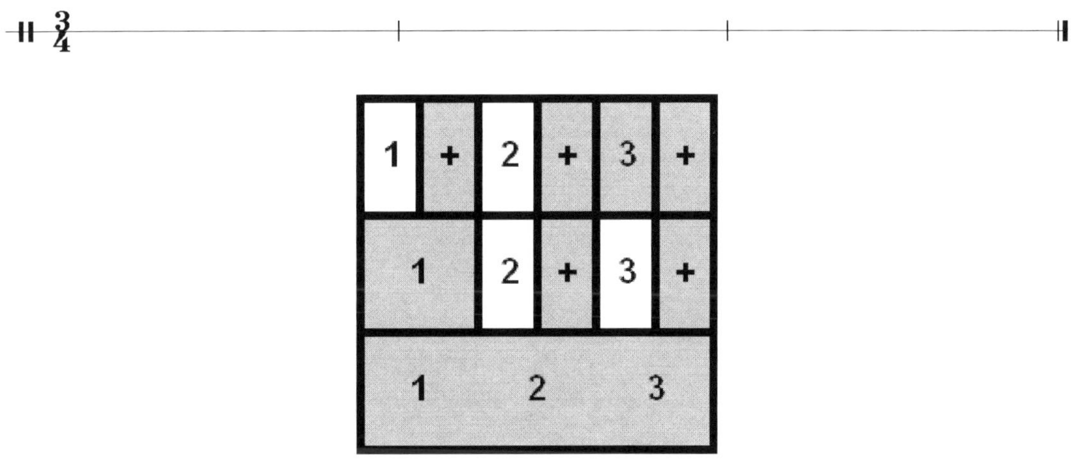

Exercise 4

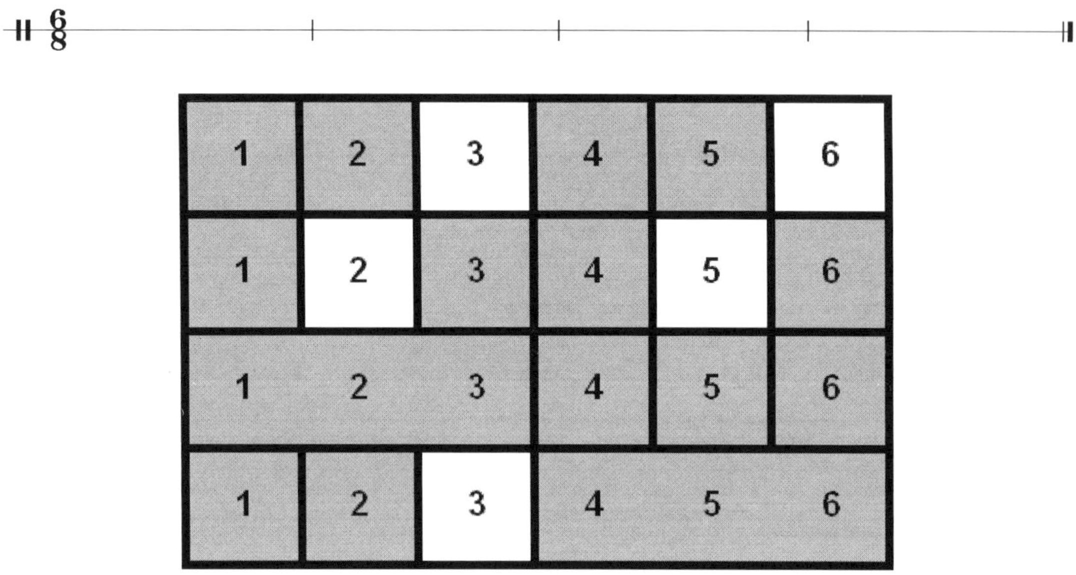

Exercise 5

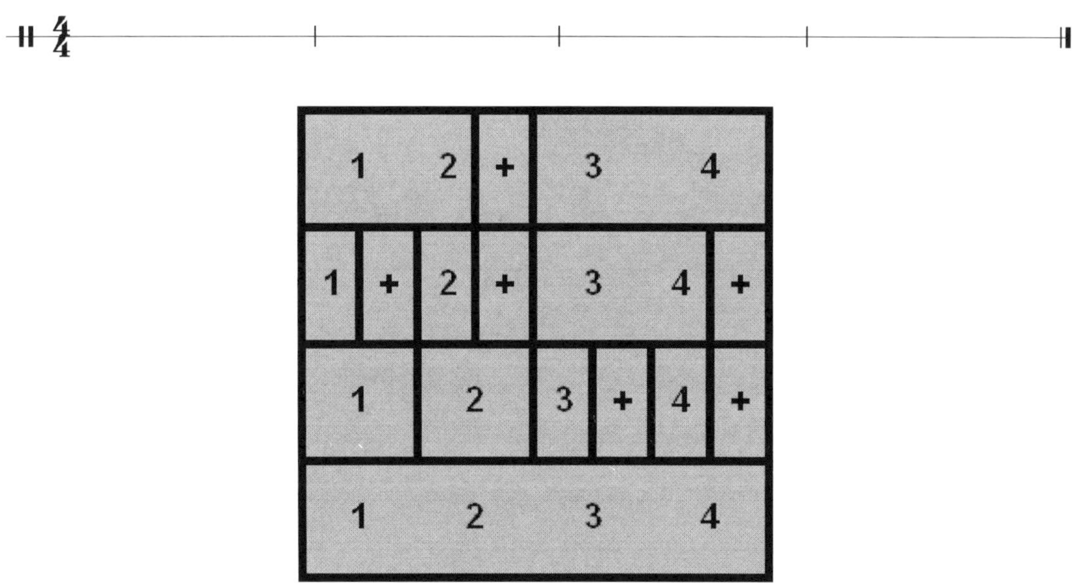

SECTION 4

Pitch & Rhythm

This section tests your ability to sight-read pitch and rhythm simultaneously

Treble Clef

The skills developed in the two previous sections are now combined to test pitch and rhythmic recognition at the same time. There are five melodic exercises for each five-note set. Practice equally with each hand.

Set A

Set B

Set C

Set D

Set E

Set F

Set G

Treble Clef - Octave Higher

The following exercises are an octave higher to improve fluency of note recognition within each set.

Set A

Set B

Set C

Set D

Set E

Set F

Set G

Bass Clef

The following exercises test pitch and rhythmic recognition in the bass clef. There are five melodic exercises for each five-note set. Practice equally with each hand.

Set A

Set G

Set F

Set E

Set D

Set C

Set B

Bass Clef - Octave Lower

The following exercises are an octave lower to improve fluency of note recognition within each set.

Set A

Set G

Set F

Set E

Set D

Set C

Set B

Beat Box Exercises - Answers

Exercise 1

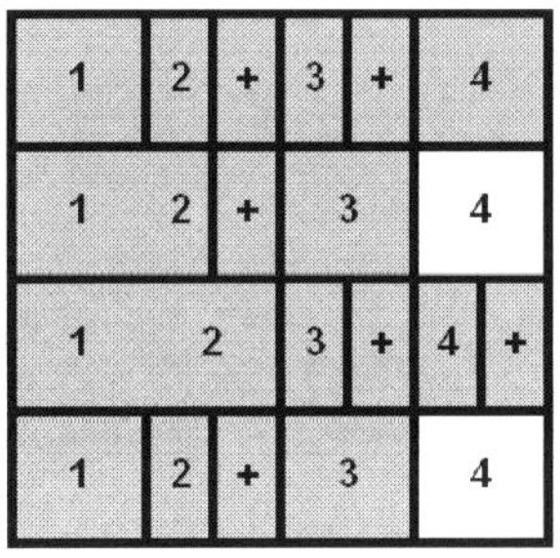

Exercise 2

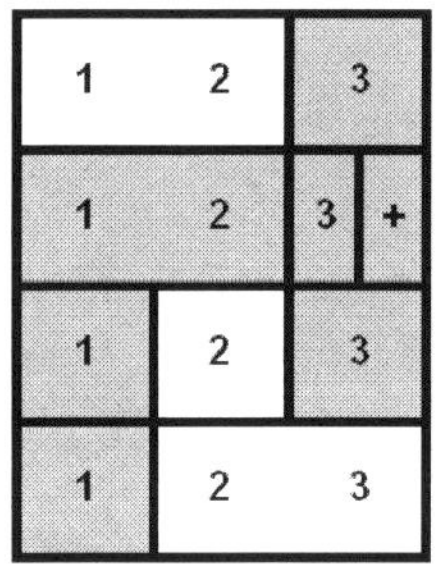

Exercise 3

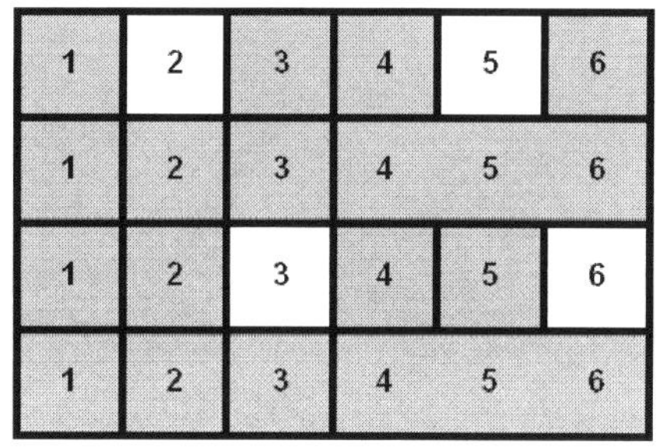

Exercise 4

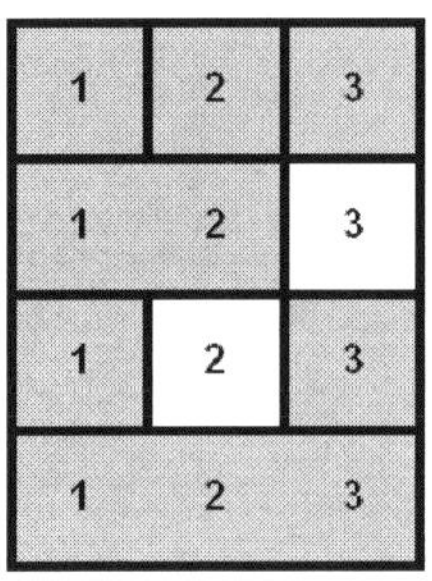

Exercise 5

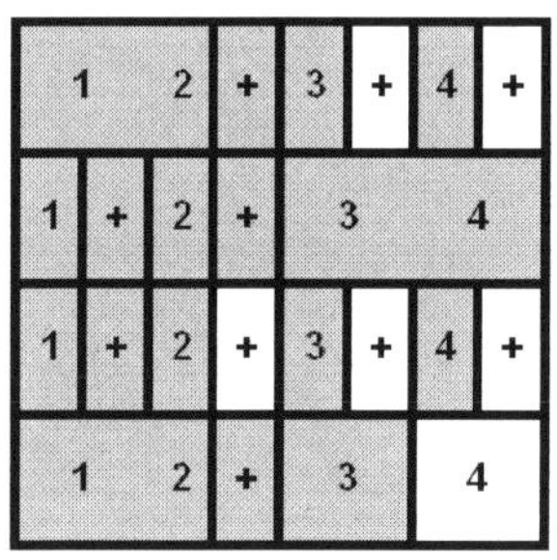

Rhythm Stave Exercises - Answers

Exercise 1

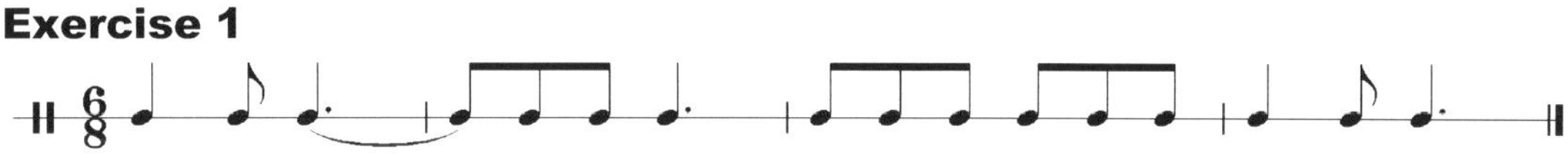

Exercise 2

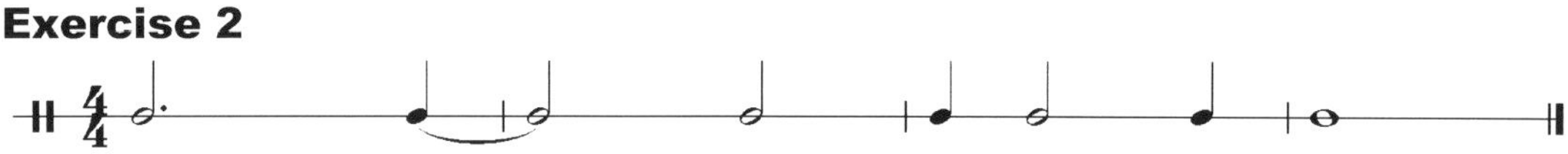

Exercise 3

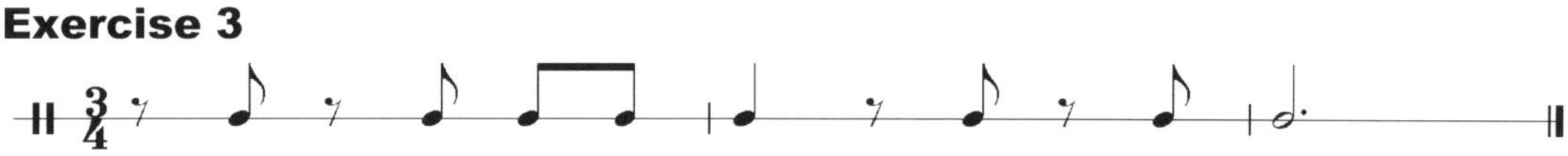

Exercise 4

Exercise 5

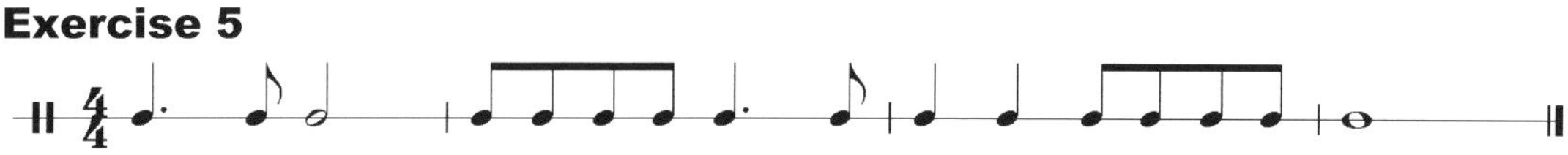